Wisdom sayings For Our Troubling Times

Words That Will Help You Take Charge of Your Life

Compiled by

Ernest S. Merrill-Boyd

With an introduction by

Dr. Sulayman Nyang, Ph.D.

Buy this book and you'll change your life.

Courtesies are extended to Guidepost, Simon & Schuster, African-American Images, Zondervan Publishers, Bantam Books, Civilized Publications, Ballantine Books and Bits & Pieces for the use of quotes of Norman Vincent Peale, David Schwartz, Michael Porter, Rick Warren, Og Mandino, Shahrazad Ali, Leo Buscaglia respectively.

If by inadvertence, any oversight has been made, the author hopes he will be forgiven for omission and will make the necessary correction at the first opportunity.

Order this book online at www.trafford.com/07-1931
or email orders@trafford.com

Most Trafford titles are also available at major online book retailers.

Note for Librarians: A cataloguing record for this book is available from Library and Archives Canada at www.collectionscanada.ca/amicus/index-e.html

ISBN: 978-1-4251-4546-0

We at Trafford believe that it is the responsibility of us all, as both individuals and corporations, to make choices that are environmentally and socially sound. You, in turn, are supporting this responsible conduct each time you purchase a Trafford book, or make use of our publishing services. To find out how you are helping, please visit www.trafford.com/responsiblepublishing.html

Our mission is to efficiently provide the world's finest, most comprehensive book publishing service, enabling every author to experience success. To find out how to publish your book, your way, and have it available worldwide, visit us online at www.trafford.com/10510

www.trafford.com

North America & international
toll-free: 1 888 232 4444 (USA & Canada)
phone: 250 383 6864 • fax: 250 383 6804 • email: info@trafford.com

The United Kingdom & Europe
phone: +44 (0)1865 487 395 • local rate: 0845 230 9601
facsimile: +44 (0)1865 481 507 • email: info.uk@trafford.co

E-mail: esmerrill@hotmail.com / ernestmerrill@yahoo.com
Tel.: 1- 268-774-5632 / 767-440-2062 / 767-285-8392

10 9 8 7 6 5 4

Introduction

Ernest S. Merrill-Boyd is an old friend who went to college with me at Hampton University in Hampton, Virginia. During those days, we read Philosophy and other courses in the social sciences. His main interest was to become a master in the humanities. He read a great deal and the collective wisdom of man in the Western world known to him. The wisdom of the elders from the Caribbean and Africa became a part of his intellectual development. Impressed by the writings of peoples of African descent and eager to familiarize himself with the Spanish and French languages and the contents of that part of the world, he served as an effective interpreter of the Romance world.

This book of his which is relevant in our time, is a collection of wisdom sayings of wise men and women and the prophets. As reflections on the human condition, this piece of literature by the author deserves our attention. Here, he is beating the drum of appeal and advising us all that we can find solutions in the challenges that life offers. Caught between the effects of pleasure and pain as categorical markers in explaining human life, the author searches carefully for the way out of this great dilemma through these wisdom sayings.

I strongly embrace this compilation of good advice by my colleague. Indeed, the advice found in this book echoes the wisdom recorded throughout the ages. I urge you to start with what you know and build on what you have been given.

Sulayman S. Nyang, Ph.D.
Howard University

Special Friends Last Forever

Leonard Coipel
Abdul Browne
Janice Nelson
Kathleen Richardson
Sacha Michael
Charles Byers
Raymond Lawrence
Paula Houston
Ateca Ephraim
Yvette Joseph
Terry Collier
Laurent Gilkes
Brian Ralph
Winston Ainsworth
Cindy Gordon
George-Anna Joseph
Seymour Blackman
Luther Mills
Fernando Samuel
Kimonette Marsh
Nkechi Edwards
Clarence Martin
Norris Morris Harris
Winston Jones
Janice Knight
Edwin Williams
Marion Benjamin

Muriel O'Mard
Athlyn Davis
Paget Lake
Twyla James
Vellie Rayne
Yuderky Galvez
Rosemarie Stephenson
Brian Henry
Holli Perry
Verena Roberts
Michelle Simmons
Geneva Blackmore
Andrew Perry
Isaline LeBlanc
Althea Innis Edris Michael
Ralph Prince
Lolita Spencer
Juno Spencer
Leon Shannon
Spencer Skerrit
Ishana Charles
Velex Davis Sumita Balooja
Charlesworth Martin
Carlton Lake
Teresa Tyler
Peter & Matilda Ducreay
Patsy Phillip

Charlene Selkridge
Everton Richardson
Rose-Marie Lake
Evelyn and Gerard Poponne
Alex Benjamin
Joe Richards
Mariako Clarke
Janice Knight
Jean Lawrence-Mathurin
Shurell Baptiste
Perez Mercer
Sydalinda Michael
Rhonda Stevens
Timothy Clarke
Wendy Quezada
Nyron Isaac
Sulayman Nyang
Sylvina Davis
Nadine Alphonse
Norma Greenidge
Ernest Benjamin
Samoya Kirby
Brucella Marsh
Henderson & Megan Fields
Andrea Nathaniel
Sherry Ann Kellman
Celia Colbourne

Marcia Marshall	Marsha Bembry	Henry Williams
Althea Ralph	Patrick & Wanda Byrne	Andrea Simon
Stacey McMahon	Anique Parker	Keisha "Astrid" James
Marion Benjamin	Claude Laviscount	Lucinda Tuitt
Maislyn Ashby	Jamal "Jacques" Warner	Michella Benjamin
Nicole Rogers	Donnamae Jarvis	Erica "Bernadette" Frederick
Glendina Jacobs	Fitzroy & Kronskie Ducreay	Andrew Blackman
Chane "Antoinette" Antonio	Gail Graham	Patrick McHugh
Patricia Abbott	Stacey "Thérèse" Peters	Dave Protheroe
Noble Ukonu	Lisa George	Sharon Natasha Simon
Sheila "Geneviève" Carty	Mitchell Hill	Sam Benjamin
Kenaz "Monique" Francis	Charmaine Philogène	Latechia Thomas
Sandra Meade	Janice Johnson	Nikisha "Michelle" Paul
Jacqueline Scott	Junie Samuel	Joycelyn Phillip-Browne
Nicola Hillhouse	Lorna "Nicole" Henry-Georges	Esrome "Johnny" Roberts
Valencia "Yannik" Thomas	Heike Lee	Samuel Lewis
Terri London	Tashina Adams	Kybian "André" Joseph
Nari Belle	Colleen R. Simpson	Nathaniel "Paddy" James
Rose "Rosemarie" Vesprey	Claudette Hill	Kathy Michael
Dorcia Gregory	Sarah Stuart	Kenrick Francis
Priscilla Michael	Clannis "Chantal" John	Ephraim & Greta Georges
Alinthia Burnette	Alison Archer	Gary Hosier
Claudine "Solange" Benjamin	Charmaine Hackett	Rhonda Barnes
Ira Samuel	Yvonne "Francine" Bryan	Michael & Nickey Rickaille
Ernestine Dowdie	Mumba	Yanik Henry
Anique Samuel	Cordelle Williams	Naeka Grant
Renée Phillips	Michael Benjamin	Melanie Goodwin
Gladys Samuel	Bruce Williamson	Alvin Samuel
Fatima John-Lewis	Mable Baptiste	James Attwood
Peggy Armstead	Anreka Beazer	Lauroma Joseph
Avit LaVille	Stephen Joseph	Rolston Hector
Kathleen George	Dorothy Chang	Jennifer Miller
Alphonso Elvin	Basem.K. Wassouf-Hadeed	Lois Joseph
Leiland Rogers	Shantia Henry	Loy Weste
Deborah Brookes	Susan Matthias	Frankie Nunes

Kellie Warner
Eddie Hunte
Irene Lake
Annie Benn
Olvanah Richardson
Barbara Matthews
Carlos Charles
Zita Ozuomba
Lakeisha Adams
Nathaniel Maynard
Celestine Moe
Loretta Gage
Joe & Sylvia Laurent
Rochelle Mings
Allan & Mildred Hunt
Addison Workman
Cleo Percival
Eustace & Cecelia Hill
Evangeline Punter
Shenica Phillip
Lawrence Blackman
Lornette James-Knight
Helenmae Winter
Caughtwright Pigott
Janice Dunbar
Felisha Goulbourne
Ken Richards
Laurilyn Henry
Melanie Stuart
Karen Martin
J.C. Martin
Geisha Weekes
Lyndon Browne
James Knight

Sandy Burns
Alicia Titus
Matika Martin
Fellisa Simon
Kia Fernandez
S.V. & Vanaja V. Raj
Claudette Samuel
Jernealia Isaac
Connie & Wendy Nicholas
Joycelyn Francis
Emelinda Miledy Torres
Ithlane Baptiste
Bongo Daley
Enroy Baltimore
Shemeke DeSilva
Charlene Benjamin
Rolston Rawlins
Seth George
Elizabeth Watkins
Cecil Wade
Marlon Charles
Priscilla Leonce
Alicia Smith
Ernest & Marilyn Piper
Koran Kong
Shakelia Riley
Arielle Mills
Vivia Ingram
Kareem Greaux
Frank De Abreu
Cordel Josiah
Vashtina Piggott
Monique Henry
Jamilla Kirwan

Joanne Adams
Gregson & Absatou Williams
Kishma Joseph
Marvel Hewitt
Laurel Martin
Shantal Liverpool
Kenyatta Thomas
Daverson Welsh
Michael Moe
Kathleen Parker
Yolanda Peters
Lesroy Merchant
Semone Ambrose
J. Nerissa Percival
Robin Edmonds
Sonnie Blaize
Debbie Theodore
Rupert Dyer
Denny Grant
Samantha Jackson
Ladesa James
Orna Walker
Charles "Max" Fernandez
Cynthia Baptiste
Geanroy Browne
Mitelbeth Thomas
Rochelle Anthony
Dee Dee Frederick
Gail Melvin
St. Clair Williams
Edwin Maatrijk
Cheryl Michael
Conrad Luke
Walton Theodore

For My daughters

Talitta & Tammy

Contents

Acknowledgements

I am deeply indebted to Arklyn Hopkins for providing me with the encouragement, inspiration and some of the material in the compilation of this book.

I am also indebted to Tracey Browne, Gary and Suzanne Hatten for their editorial comments and suggestions and Ursula Van Rensburg-Michael for her critique, editorial evaluation, provision of some of the material and motivation which greatly aided in the completion of the work.

Subject Index

Foreword

"Wisdom Sayings for Our Troubling Times" was carefully selected and compiled for those of us who sometimes go through unbalanced spiritual moments we sometimes have to endure. At times, we feel depressed for valid reasons and sometimes for no reason. Most times we are confused and don't know what to do. We sometimes have to endure rejection but remember *"Rejection is not a reflection of your self-worth"*.

We need to go beyond ourselves and immerge ourselves into deep and powerful Spiritual Meditation. The secret is the content feeling of living and experiencing Harmony and Spiritual Balance. Be at peace with yourself and those around you. For what we feel we transcend into the universe. Every negative vibration we send out, comes back two fold and every positive vibration, comes back tenfold.

When you fall off the bike, just get back on and ride it again.

So, it is with commitment, determination and passion that we move forward and gain favorable results.

"Wisdom Sayings for Our Troubling Times" does not only provide man's wisdom and insight but also the wisdom and guidance of God. This book is easy reference and a welcome break to the every day rat-race and our troubling times.

Indulge! Don't be afraid because if the sea is always smooth, you will never become a skillful sailor.

The author, my friend and mentor is compassionate, daring and free to indulge in the beauty of life!

Explore the pages within and you will be spiritually empowered.

Ursula Van Rensburg-Michael

A Special Dedication

For

Ursula Van Rensburg-Michael

Arklyn Hopkins, Michael Ozuomba, Natalie Charles, Patricia Best, Gary & Suzanne Hatten, Tracey Browne, Francine Retemyer, Angel Ramos, Sir James and Lady Emma Carlisle, Michael Browne, Hezekiah Lewis, Aliena Browne, José V.A. Humphreys, Denys Hoyte, Antoinette Berrian, Shaunah Simon, Cosmo and Gwen Jacobs, Oliver Martin, Bernard S. Percival

&

Peter and Carol-Ann Gomes

How to get the most out of this book

1. Commit yourself to read and memorize the quotations that apply to your personal condition and need and let it be like a daily mantra.

2. For good results and spiritual empowerment, review this book once a week.

3. Apply the advice from these quotations at every opportunity. Let it be a tool in dealing with life daily challenges.

4. Make a periodic check on your progress.

5. Make notes in the back of the this book on your progress when you have applied the wisdom of these quotations. Then put the date when you started and the date of your accomplishment.

Best Wishes

Wisdom sayings – Ernest S. Merrill-Boyd

Part One

Achievement

"The roots of true achievement is to become the best that you can become."

HAROLD TAYLOR

"If you can imagine it, you can achieve it. If you can dream it, you can become it."

WILLIAM ARTHUR WARD

Action

"Never do anything without considering the consequences"

Adversity

"Adversity causes some to break, others to break record."

Affirmation

"Spend your life lifting people up, not putting people down."

"Kind words can be short and easy to speak but their echoes are truly endless."

Age

"Show respect for the elderly and honour them. Reverently obey me for I am the Lord."

LEVITICUS 19:32

"Years do not make wise men; they only make old men."

MADAME SWETCHINE

"Grecian women counted their age from their marriage not from their birth."

HOMER

"While one finds company in himself and his pursuits, he cannot feel old, no matter what his years may be."

AMOS BRONSON ALCOTT

Aging

"Forget about your age and live your life."

NORMAN VINCENT PEALE

"Middle age is when your broad mind and narrow waist begin to change places."

E. JOSEPH COSSMAN

"Do not go gentle into that good night. Old age should burn and rage at close of day."

DYLAN THOMAS

Ambition

"Be ashamed to die if you haven't done anything in this life."

VOLTAIRE

Anger

"Oppose not rage while it is in its force but give it way a while and let it waste."

WILLIAM SHAKESPEARE

"Soft words turn away wrath"

Animals

"A good person takes care of his/her animals but wicked people are cruel to theirs."

PROVERBS 12:10

Anxiety

"A man who suffers before it is necessary, suffers more than is necessary."

SENECA

Arguments

"When an argument flares up, the wise person quenches it with silence."

Anonymous

Arrogance

"Nothing in the world is more haughty than a man of moderate capacity when once raised to power."

Baron Wessenburg

Association

"If you lie down with dogs, you will get up with fleas"

Spanish proverb

"Birds of a feather flock together."

Aristotle

Attitude

"Our lives are not determined by what happens to us but by how we react to what happens; not by what life brings to us but by the attitude we bring to life. A positive attitude causes a chain reaction of positive thoughts, events and outcomes. It is a catalyst, a spark that creates extraordinary results." Anon

"Alter your attitude and you can alter your life."

Unknown

"You may have to fight a battle more than once to win it."

MARGARET THATCHER

Backside

"You cannot appreciate your bottom until you sit on a pin."

ANONYMOUS

Belief

"Drugs are not always necessary, but belief in recovery always is."

NORMAN COUSINS

"Belief is the thermostat that regulates what we accomplish in life."

DR. DAVID J. SCHWARTZ

"They can conquer who believe they can."

VIRGIL

Black Culture

"We have too many hot boys, bad boys, rude boys, toy boys, play boys but not enough MEN."

MICHAEL PORTER

"When you control a man's thinking, you do not have to worry about his actions. You do not have to tell him to stand here or go yonder. He will find his "proper place" and will stay in it. You do not need to send him to the back door. He will go without being told. In fact, if there is no back door, he will cut one for his special

benefit. His education makes it necessary."

CARTER G. WOODSON

"History shows that it does not matter who is in power….those who have not learned to do for themselves and have to depend solely on others never obtain any more rights or privileges in the end than they did in the beginning."

CARTER G. WOODSON

"We value others and empower others who are not black like us but never ourselves."

E.S MERRILL-BOYD

Blunders

"Wealth without work,
Science without humanity,
Politics without principles
Pleasure without conscience
Commerce without reality
Worship without sacrifice
Rights without responsibilities
Knowledge without character."

MAHATMA GANDHI

Books

"Except for a living man, there is nothing more wonderful than a book. A book is a message to us from human souls we never saw. And yet these books arouse us, terrify us, teach us, comfort us, open our hearts to us as brothers."

CHARLES KINGSLEY

Bribery

"Judges and senators have been bought with gold."

ALEXANDER POPE

"Corrupt judges (politicians) accept secret bribes and then justice is not done."

PROVERBS 17:23

Business

"The purpose of business is to create and keep a customer."

PETER DRUCKER

Change

"The price of doing the same thing is far higher than the price of change."

WILLIAM "BILL" JEFFERSON CLINTON

Character

"Character building begins in your infancy and continues until death."

FRANKLIN D. ROOSEVELT

"Never educate a child to be a gentleman or a lady but to be a man or a woman."

HERBERT SPENCER

"Character is built out of circumstances.—From exactly the same materials one man builds palaces, while another builds hovels."

GEORGE HENRY LEWES

"Not education but character is man's greatest need and man's greatest safeguard."

HERBERT SPENCER

"A smooth sea never makes a skillful mariner."

"Great souls have wills, feeble ones have only wishes."

"Bad company corrupts good character."

"Be the change you want to see in the world."

MAHATMA GANDHI

"Your character is essentially the sum of your habits."

RICK WARREN

"If the roots are deep and strong, the tree needn't worry about the wind."

"The highest reward for a man's toil is not what he gets for it but what he becomes by it."

JOHN RUSKIN

"There is no such thing as a "self-made" person. We are made up of thousands of others. Every one who has ever done a kind deed for us or spoken one word of encouragement to us, has entered into the make-up of our character and our thoughts as well as our success."

GEORGE MATTHEW ADAMS

"Character is a victory, not a gift."

ANONYMOUS

"When the character of a person is not clear to you, look at his friends."

JAPANESE PROVERB

Charity

"He who receives a benefit should never forget it. He who bestows one should never remember it."

PIERRE CHARRON

Childhood

"Better to build a child than to repair a man."

"The first duty to children is to make them happy. If you have not made them so, you have wronged them. No other good they may get can make up for that."

CHARLES BUXTON

Children

"If you want children to keep their feet on the ground, put some responsibility on their shoulders."

ABIGAIL VAN BUREN

"Your children will become what you are; so be what you want them to be.

DAVID BLY

"Children need love, especially when they do not deserve it."

HAROLD HULBERT

"A child becomes an adult when he realizes that he has a right not only to be right but also to be wrong."

THOMAS SZASZ

"If we are to have real peace, we must begin with the children."

MAHATMA GANDHI

"Children learn what they live."

DOROTHY LAW NOLTE

"A child needs a model, not a critic."

"Your children are not your children,
They are the sons and daughters of Life's longing for itself.
They come through you but not from you,
And though they are with you they belong not to you.
You may give them your love but not your thoughts,
For they have their own thoughts.
You may house their bodies but not their souls,
For their souls dwell in the house of tomorrow, which you cannot visit, not even in your dreams.
You may strive to be like them, but seek not to make them like you.
For life goes not backward nor tarries with yesterday.

KALIL GIBRAN, THE PROPHET

Christianity

"Going to church doesn't make you a Christian any more than going to a garage makes you a car."

W.A. "BILLY" SUNDAY

"The Christian life is not merely knowing or hearing but doing the will of Christ."

FREDERICK WILLIAM ROBERTSON

"The duty of every Christian is to be a rebel."

ST. THOMAS AQUINAS

"As Christians, we must give hope to society."

FATHER GEORGE WILLIAMS

"A Christian must be tested outside the church, not inside the church."

FATHER GEORGE WILLIAMS

Church

"The Church has a moral responsibility to be the conscience of the people. How can you praise the police if they are stealing. We are not Court jesters who must just praise and praise."

JAIME CARDINAL SIN

Circumstances

"Man is not the creature of circumstances. Circumstances are the creatures of men."

BENJAMIN DISRAELI

Civility

"If you would civilize a man, begin with his grand mother."

VICTOR HUGO

Cleanliness

"Cleanliness is close to godliness."

JOHN WESLEY

Commitment

"Agreements consists of papers with signatures written on them. They mean nothing. They do not honour commitment."

Committee

"A committee is a group that keeps minutes and loses hours."

MILTON BERLE

Communication

"Examine what is said, not him who speaks."

ARABIAN PROVERB

"The reason why we have two ears and one tongue is because we should listen more and talk less."

AFRICAN PROVERB

"Problems would lessen if people would listen."

Compassion

"To live the life of a Christian with integrity and compassion , every person must be concerned with the needs of his/her neighbour."

CAMILO TORRES

"The test of our progress is not whether we add more to the abundance of those who have much; it is whether we provide enough for those who have too little."

FRANKLIN DELANO ROOSEVELT

"Comfort the feeble minded, support the weak, be patient toward all persons."

THESSALONIANS 5:14

Conceit

"Conceit is God's gift to little men."

BRUCE BARTON

Confidence

"Trust yourself. You know more than you think you do."

BENJAMIN SPOCK

Conscience

"Our life begins to end the day we become silent about things that matter."

THE REV. DR. MARTIN LUTHER KING JR.

Consistency

"A consistent man believes in destiny, a capricious man in chance."

BENJAMIN DISRAELI

"A person who removes a mountain, does so by taking away small stones."

CHINESE PROVERBS

"You can practice any virtue erratically but nothing consistently without courage."

MAYA ANGELOU

Consumerism

"Consumers are statistics. Customers are people."

STANLEY MARCUS

Corruption

"Corruption perverts justice."

JEREMY POPE

"The mind grows narrow in proportion as the soul grows corrupt."

JEAN JACQUES ROUSSEAU

"In proportion, as nations become more corrupt, more disgrace will attach to poverty and more respect to wealth."

CALEB C. COLTON

"Corruption distorts economic and social development by engendering wrong choices and by encouraging competition in bribery rather than in the quality and prices of goods and services. It has been described as a cancer. It violates public confidence in the state...."

JEREMY POPE

Conviction

"A leader has the vision and conviction that a dream can be achieved. He inspires the power and energy to get it done."

Ralph Nader

Courage

"It is not the size of the dog in the fight but the size of the fight in the dog."

Roosevelt

"The greatest pleasure in life is doing what people say you cannot do."

Walter Bagehot

"It is never too late to be what you might have been."

George Eliot

Cowardice

"To see what is right and not do it, is want of courage."

Confucius

Creativity

"Creativity requires the courage to let go of certainties."

Erich Fromm

Credit

"Neither a lender nor a borrower be."

WILLIAM SHAKESPEARE

Creditor

"Creditors have better memories than debtors."

BENJAMIN FRANKLIN

"You ask me for credit. I don't give you.—You vex.
You ask me for credit. I give you. You don't pay.— I vex.
So better you vex than I vex."

ANTIGUAN PROVERB

Criticism

"Criticism is a person's greatest test of maturity, conviction and commitment to his/her vision."

"If you do not want to be criticized, then decide to do nothing in life."

Cruelty

"Man's inhumanity to man makes countless thousands mourn."

ROBERT BURNS

Death

"When you leave your house, you can never be sure, if you will ever return."

CATHERINE ST. JEAN

"Some people are so afraid to die, that they never begin to live."

HENRY VAN DYKE

"There is no better armor against the shafts of death than to be busied in God's service."

FULLER

"He whom the gods love, dies young."

MENANDER

Debt

"A small debt produces a debtor, a large one an enemy."

PUBLIUS SYRUS

Deception

"Oh what a tangled web we weave, when first we practice to deceive."

SIR WALTER SCOTT

"Those who plot the deception of others often fall themselves."

PHAEDRUS THRACE OF MACEDONIA

Deeds

"When a man dies, people ask 'What property has he left behind?' But the angels as they bend over his grave, inquire 'What good deeds has thou sent on before thee?'

MOHAMMED

Democratic values

"A generation that acquires knowledge without ever understanding how that knowledge can benefit the community is a generation that is not learning what it means to be citizens in a democracy."

ELIZABETH HOLLANDER

Destiny

"First of all, although men have a common destiny, each individual also has to work out his own personal salvation for himself in fear and trembling. We can help one another to find the meaning of life no doubt. But in the last analysis, the individual person is responsible for living his own life and for "finding himself". If he persists in shifting his responsibility to somebody else, he fails to find out the meaning of his own experience. You cannot tell me who I am and I cannot tell you who you are. If you do not know your own identity, who is going to identify you?"

THOMAS MERTON

"We are the captains of our souls and the guardians of our destiny."

Determination

"The spirit, the will to win and the will to excel are the things that endure. These qualities are so much more important than the events that occur."

VINCE LOMBARDI

"The difference between the impossible and the possible lies in a person's determination."

TOMMY LASORDA

"See it, believe it and never give up on it."

ARNOLD SCHWARZENEGGER

"It is common sense to try something even if it fails. If it fails, try another but try something."

FRANKLIN D. ROOSEVELT

"Nothing is impossible. It is often merely for an excuse that we say things are impossible."

FRANÇOIS DE LA ROCHEFOUCAULD

"Never, never, never, ever give up."

WINSTON CHURCHILL

Dictatorship

"You can build a throne with bayonets but you cannot sit on it for long."

Discipline

"Discipline is not something that is done to the child; it is something that is done for the child."

JAMES DOBSON

Doctors

"Doctors die too."

DR. CONRAD F. STEVENS

"Better go without medicine than call in an unskilled physician."

JAPANESE PROVERB

Double Standards

"The way of the world is to praise dead saints and persecute living ones."

NATHANIEL HOWE

Doubts

"Our doubts are traitors and make us lose the good we often might win by fearing to attempt."

WILLIAM SHAKESPEARE

Dreams

"Hold fast to dreams, for if dreams die, life is a broken winged bird that cannot fly."

LANGSTON HUGHES

"Everything starts as somebody's daydreams."

Drunkenness

"There is a devil in every berry of the grape."

THE KORAN

"A drunkard is the annoyance of modesty; the trouble of civility; the spoil of wealth; the distraction of reason. He is the brewer's agent; the tavern and ale-house benefactor; the beggar's companion; the constable's trouble; his wife's woe; his children's sorrow; his neighbour's scoff; his own shame."

THOMAS ADAMS

Education

"Education is the most powerful weapon you can use to change the world."

NELSON MANDELA

"Education begins in the cradle."

THOMAS COGAN

"Education begins at the mother's knee and every word spoken in the hearing of little children tends toward the formation of their character."

HOSEA BALLOU

"Do not ask if a man has been through college. Ask if college has been through him."

EDWIN H. CHAPIN

"Education does not begin with the alphabet but with a mother's

look, a father's nod of approbation or a sign of reproof, with thoughts directed in sweet and kindly tones and words to nature, to beauty, to acts of benevolence to deeds of virtue and to the source of all good to God himself."

ANON

"Education is the most powerful tool a woman can have."

IRENE KHAN

"The brain is the most powerful weapon."

FIDEL CASTRO

"The mere imparting of information is not education. Above all things, the effort must result in making a man think and do for himself just as the Jews have done in spite of universal persecution."

CARTER G. WOODSON

"The chief difficulty with the education of the Blackman is that it has been largely imitation resulting in the enslavement of his mind."

CARTER G. WOODSON

"When a boy comes to school without knowing his lesson, he should be studied instead of being punished."

CARTER G. WOODSON

"Education is the door to freedom."

OPRAH WINFREY

Efficiency

"By being active, we are doubling our efficiency. By being inactive, we are hiding our efficiency."

AUTHOR UNKNOWN

"Reorganizing can be a wonderful method for creating the illusion of progress while producing confusion, inefficiency and demoralization."

PETRONIUS ARBITER

Emotions

"Men as well as women are much oftener led by their hearts than by their understanding."

LORD CHESTERFIELD

Endurance

"In the depth of winter, I finally learned that within me there lay an invisible summer."

ALBERT CAMUS

Enthusiasm

"A man can succeed at almost anything for which he has unlimited enthusiasm."

Envy

"Keep away from people who try to belittle your ambitions. Small people always do that but the really great make you feel that you too can become great."

MARK TWAIN

"As a moth gnaws a garment, so does envy consume a man."

CHRYSOSTOM

"The envious man grows lean at the success of his neighbour."

HORACE

Evil

"The world is in greater peril from those who tolerate evil than those who commit it." Albert Einstein

"To be free from evil thoughts is God's best gifts."

AESCHYLUS

"We cannot do evil to others without doing it to ourselves."

JOSEPH FRANCIS DESMAHIS

Example

"There is nothing so powerful as example. We put others straight by walking straight ourselves."

TAMMY V. MERRILL

"Example is more forcible than precept. People look at my six days in the week to see what I mean on the seventh."

RICHARD CECIL

"I am satisfied that we are less convinced by what we hear than by what we see."

HERODUTUS

"Live with wolves and you will learn to howl."

SPANISH PROVERB

"Not the cry but the flight of the wild duck leads the flock to fly and follow."

CHINESE PROVERB

"The people are fashioned according to the example of their king."

CLAUDIAN—LATIN POET

"There is no better sermon than a good example."

Excuses

"He that is good for making excuses is seldom good for anything else."

BENJAMIN FRANKLIN

"Often times excusing of a fault doth make a fault the worse by the excuse."

WILLIAM SHAKESPEARE

Experience

"No man was ever so completely skilled in the conduct of life as not to receive new information from age and experience."

TERRENCE- ROMAN POET

"No experience is good or bad. Treat them as lessons."

FROM THE MONKS IN THE HIMALAYAS

"You cannot have a testimony without going through a test."

UNKNOWN

Exploitation

"As long as extreme poverty exits, there will be exploitation."

JERRY NORTON

"Fishes live in the sea as men do on land. The great ones eat up the little ones."

WILLIAM SHAKESPEARE

Failure

"The downfall of a man is not the end of his life . Your past mistakes are only a small share. The bigger part of the shame is if you dwell on the past mistakes."

"Many a good man has failed because he had his wishbone where his backbone should have been."

"A failure is a person who has blundered but is not able to cash in on the experience."

ELBERT HUBBARD

"It is no disgrace to start all over. It is usually an opportunity."

Fairness

"What you do not wish others should do unto you, do not do unto them."

CONFUCIUS

Faith

"If you have faith, nothing will be impossible unto to you."

MATTHEW 17:20

"Faith is to believe what you do not yet see; the reward for this faith is to see what you believe."

ST. AUGUSTINE

Fame

"How men long for celebrity. Some would willingly sacrifice their lives for fame and not a few would rather be known by their crimes than not known at all."

SIR JOHN SINCLAIR

Fear

"A great deal of talent is lost in this world for the want of a little courage."

SYDNEY SMITH

"The one thing worst than a quitter is the person who is afraid to start."

Financial Prudence

"Do not put all your eggs in one basket."

CERVANTES

"Waste not, want not."

THOMAS HARDY

"A fool may meet with good fortune but the wise only profits by it."

DUTCH PROVERB

"Boyfriends leave, husbands die but bills remain."

D. GISELE ISAAC

"In human life, there are only two outcomes. You will either die too soon or live too long. But if you live too long, it is financial planning that will guard you against charity in old age."

UNKNOWN

"If your outgoal exceeds your income, your upkeep becomes your downfall."

Firmness

"A man must stand erect not be kept erect by others."

MARCUS AURELIUS

Fools

"It is the fool whose own tomatoes are sold to him."

AKAN PROVERB

"A fool always finds a greater fool to admire him."

NICHOLAS BOILEAU

"Young men think old men fools and old men know young men to be so."

RICHARD METCALF

"A fool may be known by six things: anger without cause; speech without profit; change without progress; inquiry without object; putting trust in a stranger; and mistaking foes for friends."

ARABIAN PROVERB

Forgiveness

"There is no future without forgiveness."

DESMOND TUTU

"We pardon as long as we love."

FRANÇOIS DE LA ROCHEFOUCAULD

Friends

"No person is your friend who demands your silence or denies your right to grow."

ALICE WALKER

"It goes without saying that your friends are usually the first to discuss your personal business behind your back."

TERRY MCMILLAN

"A friend in court is better than money in the pocket."

ANTIGUAN PROVERB

"Purchase not friends by gifts. When thou ceasest to give, such will cease to love."

FULLER

"A friend that you have to buy won't be worth what you pay for him/her, no matter what they may be."

GEORGE D. PRENTICE

"A true friend is the nectar of life."

INDIAN (TAMIL) PROVERB

"Promises may get friends but it is performance that keeps them."

"The best antique is an old friend."

"Be courteous to all, but intimate with few and let those few be well tried before you give them your confidence."

GEORGE WASHINGTON

"Without friends, no one would want to live, even if we had all other goods."

ARISTOTLE

"You can make more friends in two months by becoming interested in other people than you can in two years by trying to get other people interested in you."

DALE CARNEGIE

"When you choose your friends, don't be short-changed by choosing personality over character."

W. Somerset Maugham

Friendship

"Cut off the talk and many times you cut off the friendship."

Aristotle

"A man should keep his friendship in constant repair."

Samuel Johnson

"Be slow to fall into friendship but when thou art in, continue firm and constant."

Socrates

"The difficulty is not so great to die for a friend as to find a friend worth dying for."

Henry Home

"Two persons cannot long be friends if they cannot forgive each other's little failings."

Jean de la Bruyère

"The only way to have a friend is to be one."

Ralph Waldo Emerson

"Remembering wrongs can break up a friendship."

Proverbs 17:22

"Prosperity makes friends, adversity tries them."

"Never contract friendship with a person that is not better than thyself."

CONFUCIUS

"The holy passion of friendship is so sweet and steady and loyal and enduring in nature that it will last through a whole lifetime, if not asked to lend money."

MARK TWAIN

"Friendship is always a sweet responsibility; never an opportunity."

KHALIL GIBRAN

"It is better to be deceived by one's friends than to deceive them."

JOHANN WOLFGANG GOETHE

Games people play

"A man chases a woman until she catches him."

ANONYMOUS

Genius

"Genius is one percent inspiration and ninety-nine percent inspiration."

THOMAS A. EDISON

"Genius is only a superior power of seeing."

JOHN RUSKIN

Giving

"The most satisfying thing in life is to have been able to give a large part of one's self to others."

PIERRE TEILHARD DE CHARDIN

"The more we share, the more we have."

"Give with no strings attached and you will receive in the same manner."

Goals

"Those who do not have goals are condemned to work for those who do."

Joseph Sidaros

"To be who you are and become what you are capable of is the only goal worth living."

Alvin Ailey

"The best way to predict the future is to create it."

Anonymous

"Begin today what you are going to be from now on."

St. Jerome

"Goals are as essential to success as air is to life."

David J. Schwartz

God

"Reputation is what men and women think of us. Character is what God and angels know of us."

Thomas Paine

"We must obey God as ruler rather than politicians."

Acts 5:29

"God doesn't play dice."

ALBERT EINSTEIN

God's Grace

"I never complained of my condition but once, said an old man-when my feet were bare and I had no money to buy shoes but I met a man without feet and became contented."

Gossip

"There is only one thing worst than being talked about is not being talked about."

OSCAR WILDE

"Gossip is so tasty- how we love to swallow it."

PROVERBS 11:8

Governance

"The best of all governments is that which teaches us to govern ourselves."

JOHANN WOLFGANG GOETHE

Government

"The punishment of wise men who refuse to take part in the affairs of government is to live under the government of unwise men."

PLATO

"The government consists of a gang of men exactly like you and me. They have, taking one with another, no special talent for the business of government. They have only a talent for getting and holding office. Their principal device to that end is to seek out groups who pant and pine for something they cannot get and promise to give it to them. Nine times out of ten, that promise is worth nothing. The tenth time is made good by looting 'A' to satisfy 'B'. In other words, government is a broker in pillage and every election is sort of an advance auction sale of stolen good."

H.L. MENCKEN

Gratitude

"Be grateful for what you have, not regretful for what you haven't."

"Gratitude to God should be as regular as our heartbeat."

"Instead of counting their blessings, many people magnify their problems."

Greatness

"Nothing great will ever be achieved without great men and men are great only if they are determined to be so."

CHARLES DE GAULLE

"Some are born great, some achieve greatness and some have greatness thrust upon them."

WILLIAM SHAKESPEARE

Grief

"When you suffer loss, do not grieve as those who have no hope.

If you are holding on past hurts and pains...Let it go!"

T.D. Jakes

Grudge

"The heaviest thing a person can carry is a grudge."

Guidance

"If we acknowledge God in all our ways, he has promised safely to direct our steps and in our experience we shall find his promise fulfilled."

Edward Payson

Guilt

"The difference between guilt and shame is very clear—in theory. We feel guilty for what we do. We feel shame for what we are."

Lewis B. Smedes

Habit

"Habit is like a cable. We weave a thread of it every day and at last we cannot break it."

"There are two extremes, O brethren, which a holy man should avoid – the habitual practice of self-indulgence, which is vulgar and profitless and the practice of self-mortification which is painful and equally profitless."

THE BUDDHA

"Your feet are not big enough to walk the earth. You can only do what is right and hope some will emulate your good habits."

ANONYMOUS

"I am your constant companion. I am your greatest helper or heaviest burden. I will push you onward or drag you down to failure. I am completely at your command. Half the things you do you might just as well turn over to me and I will be able to do them quickly and correctly. I am easily managed—you must merely be firm with me. Show me exactly how you want something done and after a few lessons I will do it automatically. I am the servant of all great men; and alas, of all failures, as well. Those who are great, I have made great. Those who are failures, I have made failures. I am not a machine, though I work with all the precision of a machine plus the intelligence of a man.

You may run me for profit or run me for ruin—it makes no difference to me. Take me, train me, be firm with me and I will place the world at your feet.

Be easy with me and I will destroy you. Who am I? **I am habit.**"

ANONYMOUS

Happiness

"When you are not happy with yourself, you cannot be happy with others."

DARYL MITCHELL

"There is only one happiness in life, to love and to be loved."

GEORGE SAND

"If you are patient in one moment of anger, you will avoid one hundred days of sorrow."

CHINESE PROVERB

"If you want happiness for an hour, take a nap. If you want happiness for a day, go fishing. If you want happiness for a year, inherit a fortune. If you want happiness for a life time, help somebody."

CHINESE PROVERB

Healing

"As soon as healing takes place, go out and heal somebody else."

MAYA ANGELOU

Health

"The groundwork of all happiness is health."

"The secret of health for both mind and body is not to mourn for the past, worry about the future, or anticipate troubles but to live in the present moment and wisely."

THE BUDDHA

"Let thy medicine be thy food and thy food be thy medicine."

HIPPOCRATES

Home

"A hundred men can make an encampment but it requires a woman to make a home."

CHINESE PROVERB

"He is the happiest, be he king or peasant, who finds peace in his home."

JOHANN WOLFGANG GOETHE

"Every home where love abides and friendship is a guest, is surely home and home, sweet, home; for there the heart lies."

HENRY VAN DYKE

Honesty

"An honest man is the noblest work of God."

ALEXANDER POPE

"Honesty is one business policy that will never have to be changed to keep up with the times."

Hope

"Nothing last forever, not even your troubles."

ARNOLD H. GLASGOW

"This too shall pass."

ZULU PROVERB

"There is no winter in the kingdom of hope."

RUSSIAN PROVERB

Human Behavior

"Nothing is more hateful to a poor man than the purse-proud arrogance of the rich. But let the poor man become rich and he runs at once into the vice against which he so feelingly declaimed. There are strange contradictions in human character."

RICHARD CUMBERLAND

"If you make people think that they are thinking, they will love you but if you really make them think, they will hate you."

DON MARQUIS

"When a man beats a woman, it is domestic abuse but when a woman beats a man, it is foreplay."

ANTIGUAN HUMOR

"Human behavior is the result of training- repetitive instructions and familiarity of environment."

SHAHRAZAD ALI

Human Relation

"What do we live for if it is not to make life less difficult for each other?"

GEORGE ELIOT

Humility

"A man should never be ashamed to own he has been in the wrong which is but saying in other words that he is wiser today than he was yesterday."

ALEXANDER POPE

"A great man is always willing to be little."

Humor

"If we could spend good humor, we would live healthier."

LOPE DE VEGA

"Humor facilitates communications, strengthens immunity, alleviates pain, lessens anxiety, relaxes emotional and muscular tension and inspires creativity and hope. Just as beauty lies in the eyes of the beholder, so humour depends on the mind of the spectator."

DR. JAIME SANZ-ORTIZ

Hypocrisy

"Don't stay away from church because there are so many hypocrites. Remember, there is always room for one more."

SIR ARTHUR R. ADAMS

Idleness

"An idle brain is the devil's workshop."

ENGLISH PROVERB

"Lost time is never found again."

"We cannot waste time. We can only waste ourselves."

GEORGE MATTHEW ADAMS

Imagination

"Imagination is the voice of daring. If there is anything godlike about God is that he dared to imagine everything."

HENRY MILLER

"Imagination is the eye of the soul."

JOSEPH JOUBERT

"Imagination is everything. It is the preview of life's coming attractions."

ALBERT EINSTEIN

Industriousness

"Give work rather than alms to the poor. The former drives out laziness, the latter industry."

TRYON EDWARDS

Infidelity

"Never feed a woman for another man."

ST. LUCIAN PROVERB

"The nurse of infidelity is sensuality."

RICHARD CECIL

Influence

"We can influence others by treating them in the same manner we would like them to treat us. We are all images of each other, with the same senses, the same feelings, the same hopes, the same fears, the same faults and the same blood. If one itches, his neighbour scratches. If another smiles, her friend responds in kind."

Integrity

"When you can't change things, at least bear witness to that which is wrong."

GEORGE GALLOWAY

"Blessed is the man that does not walk in the counsel of the ungodly."

PSALM 1:1

"Always keep in private, the things told to you in confidence."

"When gain is put before integrity, society crumbles."

PAM BROWN

"The greatest need in this world is that of men who cannot be bought or sold; men that are sincere and honest in the most intimate depths of their souls; men that are not afraid to give sin the name it deserves; men whose conscience is as loyal to his duty as a compass to the North; men who stand on the side of justice even if the sky is falling."

ELLEN G. WHITE

Intelligence

"Intelligence rules the world and ignorance carries the load."

MARCUS GARVEY

Intuition

"Men have sight, women have insight."

VICTOR HUGO

Jealousy

"Don't stay long when the husband is not at home."

JAPANESE PROVERB

"In jealousy, there is more self-love than of love to another."

ROCHEFOUCAULD

"Jealousy sees things always with magnifying glasses which make little things large, of dwarfs giants, of suspicions truths."

CERVANTES

Junk food

"We are digging our graves with our teeth."

THOMAS MOFFETT

Justice

"Let every worker be given his/her just wage."

JESUS CHRIST

"An honest man nearly always thinks justly."

JEAN JACQUES ROUSSEAU

"How can a people be free that has not learned to be just."

ABBÉ SIEYES

"Justice must not only be done, it must be seen to have been done."

UNKNOWN

"It works if you are rich and powerful but ignores you if you are powerless."

Kindness

"Kindness is a language which the deaf can hear and the blind can see."

"Love thy neighbour as thyself."

JESUS CHRIST

"In this life, try to be a little kinder."

ALDOUS HUXLEY

Knowledge

"When you don't know, you don't know."

CHARLES "BOLD FACE" ISAAC

"Knowledge without wisdom is a load of books on the back of an ass."

JAPANESE PROVERB

Laughter

"The human race has one really effective weapon and that is laughter."

MARK TWAIN

"Laughter is a tranquilizer with no side effects."

Lawyers

"No person can be a sound lawyer who is not well read in the laws of Moses."

FISHER AMES

Laziness

"Go ahead and be lazy. Sleep on but you will go hungry."

PROVERBS 19:15

"Laziness and stupidity are first cousins."

ANTOINE RIVAROL

"What people want is not talent; it is purpose. In other words, not the power to achieve but the will to labour. "

EDWARD GEORGE BULWER

"You get nothing from doing nothing."

ARKLYN HOPKINS

Leadership

"Unless you are faithful in small matters, you won't be faithful in large ones."

LUKE 16:10

"A true leader is a model for his followers."

"Rank does not confer privilege or give power. It imposes responsibility."

"Cows have no business in horseplay."

JAMAICAN PROVERB

"The man who follows a crowd will never be followed by a crowd."

R.S. DONNELL

"Leadership is the special quality which enables people to stand up and pull the rest of us over the horizon."

JAMES L. FISHER

"Leadership is moving up and pulling others with you."

TIMOTHY CLARKE

"You can't lead if you don't know where you are going."

TONEY OLTON

Learning

"The purpose of learning is to change behavior. If behavior has not changed, then learning has not taken place."

E.S. MERRILL-BOYD

"If we taught children to speak, they'd never learn."

WILLIAM HULL

Lies

"If an idiot were to tell you the same story every day for a year, you would end up believing him."

EDMUND BURKE

"A truth is not hard to kill and a lie told well is immortal."

MARK TWAIN

Life

"Learn to begin again. That's life- a series of new beginnings."

TAMMY V. MERRILL

"The purpose of life, after all, is to live it, to taste experience to the utmost, to reach out eagerly and without fear for newer and richer experience."

ELEANOR ROOSEVELT

"Don't ask to have your life's load lightened...but for courage to endure;
Don't ask for fulfillment in all your life... but for patience to accept frustration;
Don't ask for perfection in all you do...but for the wisdom not to repeat mistakes;
And finally, don't ask for more...before saying 'Thank you' for what you have already received."

"Nothing in life is to be feared, it is only to be understood. Now is the time to understand more, so that we may fear less."

MARIE CURIE

"Regret for the things we did can be tempered by time; it is regret for the things we did not do that is inconsolable."

SIDNEY J. HARRIS

"Without a struggle, there can be no progress."

HELEN KELLER

"Learn from yesterday, live for today, hope for tomorrow."

"You gotta play the hand that dealt you. There may be pain in that hand but you have to play it."

JAMES BRADY

"There is no sadness in life that cannot be reversed."

ANONYMOUS

"The difficulties of life are to make us better — not bitter."

UNKNOWN

"All life is an experiment. The more experiments you make, the better."

WALDO RALPH EMERSON

Literature

"The literature of a people must spring from the sense of its nationality; and nationality is impossible without self-respect and self-respect is impossible without liberty."

HARRIET BEECHER STOWE

"The decline of literature indicates the decline of a nation; the two keep pace in their downward tendency."

JOHANN WOLGANG VON GOETHE

"A lawyer without history and literature is a mechanic, a mere working mason; if he possesses some knowledge of these, he may venture to call himself an architect."

SIR WALTER SCOTT

Losing

"Always have the situation under control, even if losing. Never betray an inward sense of defeat."

ARTHUR ASHE

Loneliness

"People are lonely because they build walls instead of bridges."

JOSEPH FORT NEWTON

Love

"Love wants to give but lust wants to get."

"If you love somebody, let them go. If they return they were always yours. If they do not, they never were."

ANON

"It is better to have loved and lost than not to have loved at all."

ALFRED TENNYSON

"Love creates an "us" without destroying the "me".

LEO BUSCAGLIA

"You can give without loving but you cannot love without giving."

RICK WARREN

"You will know the depth of a man's love by the quality of his listening."

MICHAEL PORTER

"Love does not keep a record of wrongs."

CORINTHIANS 13: 4

"Love sees through a telescope, not a microscope."

"Faults are thick where love is thin."

"A man in love mistakes a pimple for a dimple."

JAPANESE PROVERB

"If you are too busy judging people, you can't love them."

MOTHER TERESA

Loyalty

"Whose bread you eat, whose song you sing."

GERMAN PROVERB

"No one can be a slave of two masters; he will hate one and love the other; he will be loyal to one and despise the other. You cannot serve both God and money"

MATTHEW 6:24

Manners

"Manners are stronger than laws."

ALEXANDER CARLILE

Mediocrity

"Mediocrity is excellent to the eyes of mediocre people."

JOSEPH JOUBERT

Misery

"Misery loves company."

ENGLISH PROVERB

Money

"Money is everybody's business."

AFRICAN ENTREPRENEUR

"Money is the answer to all things."

ECCLESIASTES 10:19

Moods

"If you are having a bad day, get another one and get it quick."

UNKNOWN

Motherhood

"The joy of motherhood is having successful children."

"A man never sees all that his mother has been to him till it's too late to let her know that he sees it."

WILLIAM DEAN HOWELLS

Motivation

"Motivation is what gets you started. Habit is what keeps you going."

JIM RYUN

"Motivation is everything. You can do the work of two people but you can't be two people. Instead, you have to inspire the next guy down the line and get him to inspire his people."

LEE IACCOCA

"Let death be your motivator."

ARKLYN HOPKINS

Music

"Music has charms to soothe the savage beast."

WILLIAM CONGREVE

Nationhood

"The ruin of a nation begins in the home of its people."

ASHANTI PROVERB

"No nation can be destroyed while it possesses a good home life."

JOSIAH GILBERT HOLLAND

"When the women are strong, the men are weak."

CHINESE PROVERB

"Respect is what holds the bonds of a nation together."

SYRIAN PROVERB

"Without moral and intellectual independence, there is no anchor for national independence."

DAVID BEN-GURION

Necessity

"Necessity is the mother of invention."

GEORGE FARQUHAR

Obstacles

"Obstacles are those frightful things you see when you take your eyes off your goal."

Old men

"Your sailing days are over. Your harbour lights are out.
What was once your sex appeal, is now your water spout."

Opportunity

"The world owes us nothing. We have to create our own opportunities."

LESTER BRYANT BIRD

"When life gives you dung, turn it into fertilizer."

JOSEPH SIDAROS

"Ask and you will receive. Seek and you will find. Knock and it will be opened unto you."

MATTHEW 7:7

"If opportunity does not knock, build another door."

MILTON BERLE

"Opportunity, sooner or later comes to all who work and wish."

LORD STANLEY

Opposition

"Great spirits have always encountered violent opposition from mediocre minds."

ALBERT EINSTEIN

Parenting

"Human beings are the only creatures on earth that allow their children to come back."

BILL COSBY

"He that does not bring up his son to some honest calling and employment brings him up to be a thief." Jewish proverb

"Parents wonder why the streams are bitter when they themselves have poisoned the fountain."

JOHN LOCKE

Parliament

"Parliament is not a congress of ambassadors from different and hostile interests, which interest each must maintain, as an agent and advocate, against other agents and advocates; but parliament is a deliberate assembly of one nation, with one interest, that of the whole, where not local purposes, not local prejudices ought to guide but the general good, resulting from the general reason of the whole. You choose a member indeed, but when you have chosen him, he is not a member of Bristol, but a Member of Parliament."

EDMUND BURKE

Patience

"Be patient with everyone but above all with yourself."

ST. FRANCIS DE SALES

"The key to everything is patience. You get the chicken by hatching the eggs, not by smashing it open."

ARNOLD H. GLASGOW

Patriotism

"Love your country and do it no harm."

HU JINTAO

Peace of Mind

"Being cheerful keeps you healthy. It is slow death to be gloomy all the time."

PROVERBS 17:22

"Thou will keep him in perfect peace whose mind in stayed on thee."

ISAIAH 26: 3,4

"Possession of material riches without inner peace is like dying of thirst while bathing in the river."

PARAMHANSA YOGANANDA

"Do not carry your troubles into another day. Let them set with the sun."

CLAUDINE BENJAMIN

Perception

"It is the mind that maketh good of ill, that maketh wretch or happy, rich or poor."

EDMUND SPENCER

"We don't see things as they are. We see things as we are."

ANAÏS NIN

"What you see is what you get."

FLIP WILSON

"The way you see your life shapes your life."

RICK WARREN

"It's not what people say to you; it is what you say to yourself that matters."

ARKLYN HOPKINS

Perseverance

"The glory is not in never failing but in rising every time you fall."

CHINESE PROVERB

"Give us grace Oh God to dare to do the deed which we well know cries to be done.

Let us not hesitate because of ease, or the words of people's mouth, or our own lives.

Mighty causes are calling us—the freeing of women, the training of children, the putting down of hate and poverty and *exploitation*—all these and more. But they call with voices that mean work and sacrifice and death. May we find a way to meet the task."

W.E. DUBOIS

"I am not discouraged because every wrong attempt discarded is another step forward."

THOMAS A. EDISON

"I have not failed. I have just found 10,000 ways that don't work."

THOMAS A. EDISON

"The man who removes a mountain begins by carrying away small stones."

CHINESE PROVERB

"No pain, no gain, no thorns, no throne, no gall, no glory, no cross, no crown."

WILLIAM PENN

"The longest journey begins with the first step."

CHINESE PROVERB

"The man or woman who can drive himself/herself further once the effort gets painful is the man or woman who will win."

ROGER BANNISTER

"Great works are performed not by strength but perseverance."

SAMUEL JOHNSON

"If a man doesn't attempt more than he can possibly do, he will never know all that he can do."

HAILE SELASSIE

"We can do anything we want to do if we stick to it long enough."

HELEN KELLER

"By perseverance, the snail reached the ark."

"The mightiest oak was once a little nut that held its ground."

Persistence

"That which we persist in doing becomes easier to do. Not that the nature of the thing has changed but that our ability to do has increased."

RALPH WALDO EMERSON

Pioneering

"Do not follow the path. Go where there is no path to begin the trail."

ASHANTI PROVERB

Pleasure

"Every nerve that thrills with pleasure can also agonize with pain."

HORACE MANN

Planning

"Proper preparation prevents poor performance."

"No wind makes for him that hath no intended port to sail unto."

MICHEL MONTAIGNE

"Plans are nothing, planning is everything."

GENERAL DWIGHT D. EISENHOWER

Politicians

"Instead of giving a politician the keys to the city, it might be better to change the locks."

ARNOLD H. GLASGOW

Politics

"The purpose of politics is about changing things, not climbing a greasy pole."

GEORGE GALLOWAY

"People vote their resentment, not their appreciation. The average person does not vote for anything but against something."

WILLIAM BENNETT MUNRO

"If you wish the support of the broad masses, you must tell them the crudest and most stupid things."

ADOLF HITLER

"Two kinds of men generally best succeed in political life; men of no principle but of great talent; and men of no talent but of one principle—that of obedience to their superiors."

"A politician who is weak and friendly in the right is no match for a politician tenaciously and pugnaciously in the wrong."

EDWIN PERCY WHIPPLE

"Politics is a profession; a serious, complicated and in its true sense, a noble one."

GENERAL DWIGHT D. EISENHOWER

"He that has much, much is expected of him"

"The people can have anything they want. The trouble is they do not want anything because that's the way they vote on election day."

EUGENE V. DEBS

"The working class can kiss my arse. I've got a foreman's job at last."

ENGLISH PROVERB

"In Antigua, the only thing that is sweeter than sugar cake is politics."

VERNON EDWARDS SR.

"Politics should not be used as a tool of discord but as a unifying force to empower people."

E.S. MERRILL-BOYD

"The more things change, the more they remain the same."

FRENCH PROVERB

"You cannot put the people's business forward unless you drain the swamp *of corruption.*"

NANCY PELOSI

"Everybody in politics lies, but they do with such ease, it's troubling."

DAVID GEFFEN

"When bad men combine, the good must associate, else they will fall one by one."

EDMUND BURKE

Positive Thinking

"We are what we think. All that we are arises with our thoughts. With our thoughts we can make our world."

THE BUDDHA

"Think positive and you will perform positive so you achieve positive results."

AUTHOR UNKNOWN

"Always think thoughts of faith and courage, not defeat and ineffectiveness."

NORMAN VINCENT PEALE

"Think positive and you will perform positive so you achieve positive results."

AUTHOR UNKNOWN

"What you think means more than anything else in your life. More than what you earn, more than where you live, more than your social position and more than what anyone else may think about you."

GEORGE MATTHEW ADAMS

Poverty

"Poverty is not an act of God but an act of greedy men."

"If you think poor, you are poor."

WALLY AMOS

"He/She is poor whose expenses exceed his/her income."

JEAN DE LA BRUYÈRE

"A man who works for another man will never get rich."

ANDREW CARNEGIE

"Wise people live in wealth and luxury but stupid people spend their money as fast as they get it."

PROVERBS 21:20

Power

"Absolute power corrupts absolutely"

LORD ACTON

"Power acquired by guilt has seldom been directed to any good end or useful purpose."

TACITUS

"No man is wise enough nor good enough to be trusted with unlimited power."

CALEB COLTON

"Man proposes and God disposes."

THOMAS À KEMPIS

"He who controls the economy is he who dictates the politics."

LEO HUBERMAN

"He who pays the piper can call the tune."

ENGLISH PROVERB

Pride

"Don't let your pride become inflated.—you may have to swallow it someday."

"A man performs nothing in which to take pride if he first does not take pride in himself."

THOMAS WATSON

Problems

"Be thankful for problems. If they were less difficult, someone with less ability might have your job."

BITS & PIECES

Procrastination

"Never put off till tomorrow that which you can do today."

BENJAMIN FRANKLIN

Professionalism

"A professional is someone who can do his best work when he doesn't feel like it."

ALISTAIR COOKE

Promises

"Promises are comfort to a fool"

PROVERBS

Purpose

"The man without a purpose is like a ship without a rudder—a waif, a nothing, a no man."

THOMAS CARLYLE

"People have to feel needed. Frequently, we just offer a job and 'perks'. We don't always offer people a purpose. When people feel there is a purpose and that they are needed, there is not much else to do except let them do the work."

MAYA ANGELOU

Reading

"Our lives are too short to experience everything, so we have to read the experiences of others through autobiographies, biographies and history."

MARCUS GARVEY

Reason

"The absence of reason results into war."

FRANCISCO JOSÉ DE GOYA

Recognition

"If you don't blow your horn, it will get rusty."

DR. ERIC WILLIAMS

"Squeaking wheels get the most grease."

UNKNOWN

"Recognition is the greatest motivator."

GERARD C. EAKEDALE

Rejection

"Don't be afraid of rejection because there is a lot of it in the world."

WHOOPI GOLDBERG

"Rejection by others is not a reflection of your self-worth."

Relationship

"The person who seeks to change another person in a relationship basically sets the stage for a great deal of conflict."

"To understand how any society functions you must understand the relationship between the men and the women."

ANGELA DAVIS

"A relationship is placing one's heart and soul in the hands of another while taking charge of another in one's soul and heart."

KAHLIL GIBRAN

"The important things in life is people, not things. People impair relationships by putting material things first."

FRANCINE RETEMYER

"You should not make anyone your priority, if you are their option."

UNKNOWN

"If someone can't treat you right, love you back and see your worth... Let it go! Let them go!"

T.D. JAKES

Religion

"If men are so wicked with religion what would they be without it."

BENJAMIN FRANKLIN

Reputation

"The most important thing for a young man (or young woman) is to establish a credit- a reputation, character."

JOHN D. ROCKEFELLER

"If I take care of my character, my reputation will take care of itself."

DWIGHT L. MOODY

"A good reputation is sweeter than a jar of honey. "

PROVERBS

Revenge

"The best revenge is massive success."

FRANK SINATRA

Respect

"The most despicable form of respect is one that is controlled by fear."

ALBERT CAMUS

Responsibility

"It is easy to dodge our responsibilities but we cannot dodge the consequences of dodging them."

Revolution

"It is not necessary to wait until all conditions for making revolution exist; the insurrection can create them."

ERNESTO "CHE" GUEVARA

"Revolutions never last but the super super rich do."

E.S. MERRILL-BOYD

Risks

"Fortune favours the brave."

Sadness

"There is no sadness in life that cannot be reversed."

Salesmanship

"A salesman is as good as his last sale."

"Sampson killed a thousand Philistines with the jaw bone of an ass. Thousands of sales are lost every day with the same tool." Zig Zigler

Self-actualization

"Act the way you want to be and soon you will be the way you act."

DR. JOHNNIE COLEMAN

Selfishness

"A person is called selfish not for pursuing his/her own good but for neglecting his neighbour's"

RICHARD WHATELY

"Selfishness is the root and source of all natural and moral evils."

NATHANIEL EMMONS

Self-Pity

"Do not cry over spilt milk. Go milk another cow."

RUEL JAMES.

Self-Reliance

"God gives every bird its food but He does not throw it into the nest."

JOSIAH GILBERT HOLLAND

"Depend not another, but lean instead on thyself... True happiness is born of self-reliance."

MANU

Self-Respect

"Above all things, reverence yourself."

PYTHAGORAS

Self-Righteousness

"When you point your finger at someone else, you should remember that three of your fingers are pointing at you."

AFRICAN PROVERB

"The only man who never makes a mistake is the man who never does anything."

THEODORE ROOSEVELT

Self-worth

"Never settle for the crumbs of life."

OG MANDINO

"All you have to do to receive your divine inheritance is change your old way of thinking."

JOHN RANDOLPH PRICE

"Nobody can make you feel inferior without your consent."

ELEANOR ROOSEVELT

"Love not what you are but only what you may become."

CERVANTES

"If we price ourselves too low, the world will agree, but if we price ourselves with the very best, the world also willingly accepts that valuation."

OG MANDINO

"If you know what life is worth,
You would look for yours on Earth,
So now you see the light,
You should stand up for your right."

BOB MARLEY

"When you look for the good in others, you discover the best in yourself."

MARTIN WALSH

"You cannot belong to anyone else until you belong to yourself."

PEARL BAILEY

Service

"Sow good service and sweet remembrance will grow from them."

MADAME DE STAËL

"Service to humanity is the best work of life."

JAYCEES' CREED

Sincerity

"Sincerity, even if it speaks with a stutter, will sound eloquent when inspired."

EIJIE YOSHIKAWA - TAIKO

Slander

"The slanderer and the assassin differ only in the weapon they use; with the assassin, it is the dagger; with the slanderer, it is the tongue. The former is worse than the latter, for the last only kills the body, while the other murders the reputation and peace."

TRYON EDWARDS

Slavery

"Paradise is under your master's feet."

MAURITANIAN PROVERB

Small minds

"Narrow minds think nothing right that is above their own capacity."

FRANÇOIS DUC DE LA ROCHEFOUCAULD

Soul

"You need chaos in your soul to give birth to a dancing star."

FRIEDRICH NIETZSCHE

Success

"Success is the ability to go from one failure to another with no loss of enthusiasm."

WINSTON S. CHURCHILL

"A successful man is one who helps others succeed."

CONFUCIUS

"A man can succeed at almost anything for which he has unlimited enthusiasm."

"Coming together is a beginning. Keeping together is a process, working together is a success."

HENRY FORD

"Your failures in life come from not realizing your nearness to success when you give up."

YORUBA PROVERB

"Success is completing the task you have set out to do."

ARKLYN HOPKINS

"You survived 100, 000 other sperms to get here. What do you mean you don't know what to do."

LES BROWN

"The secret of success in life is for a man to be ready for his opportunity when it comes."

BENJAMIN DISRAELI

"Success is never losing hope."

HEZEKIAH A. LEWIS

"To be able to look back on one's life with satisfaction, is to live twice."

MARCUS VALERIUS MARTIALIS

"No one can cheat you out of ultimate success but yourself."

RALPH WALDO EMERSON

Suffering

"Night brings out stars as sorrow shows us truths."

GAMALIEL BAILEY

"We need to suffer that we may learn to pity."

LETITIA ELIZABETH LANDON

"He who suffers, remembers."

OG MANDINO

Teaching

"The teacher who is attempting to teach without inspiring the pupil with a desire to learn is hammering a cold iron."

HORACE MANN

Temper

"Temper if ungoverned, governs the whole man."

ANTHONY SHAFTESBURY

Temptation

"I see the devil's hook and yet cannot help nibbling at his bait."

MOSES ADAMS

Thinking

"Thinking is the hardest work there is which is the probable reason why so few engage in it."

HENRY FORD.

"Those who have finished by making others think with them have usually been those who began by daring to think for themselves."

CALEB C. COLTON

"The way you think determines the way you feel."

"We are what we think. All that we are arises with our thoughts. With our thoughts we can make our world."

THE BUDDHA

"The thinking that guides your intelligence is more important than the size of your intelligence."

DR. DAVID J. SCHWARTZ

Thoughts

"Great men are they who see that spiritual is stronger than any material force—that thoughts rule the world."

RALPH WALDO EMERSON

"Learning without thought is labour lost. Thought without learning is dangerous."

CONFUCIUS

Time

"Time brings all things to pass."

AESHYLUS

"Always in motion is the future."

YODA, STAR WARS EPISODE

Trouble

"The little troubles and worries of life so many of which we meet, may be as stumbling blocks in our way or we may make them stepping stones to a noble character and to Heaven."

"Troubles are often the tools by which God fashions us for better things."

HENRY WARD BEECHER

Trust

"I would rather walk with God in the dark than go alone in the light."

MARY GARDINER BRAINARD

"Trust God for great things; with your five loaves and two fishes, He will show you a way to feed thousands."

HORACE BUSHNELL

"To be trusted is a greater compliment than to be loved."

J. MacDonald

"Take special care that thou never trust any friend or servant with any matter that may endanger thine estate. For so shalt thou make thyself a bondslave to him that thou trustest and leave thyself always to his mercy."

Sir Walter Raleigh

Truth

"In a time of universal deceit, telling the truth is a revolutionary act."

Anonymous

"The greatest homage we can pay to truth is to use it."

Ralph Waldo Emerson

Unity

"Two are better off than one, because together they can work more effectively. If one of them falls down, the other can help him up... Two people can resist an attack that would defeat one person alone. A rope made of three cords is hard to break."

Ecclesiastes 4:9

"A single arrow is easily broken but not ten in a bundle."

Japanese proverb

Victory

"One may know how to gain a victory and not know how to use it."

PEDRO CALDERÓN DE LA BARCA

Vision

"People of vision see the world, while others see the village."

"It is easy to see but it is harder to foresee."

BENJAMIN FRANKLIN

Water

A lesson to learn from water

"It offers direct resistance to nothing but flows around all things. It will erode anything that stands in its way for long. With its character of flowing over, under, on the sides, in front, in the back and through anything which it crosses, it is almost impossible to stop. Remember that whenever its flows stop, it starts to stagnate.
Our lives should be lived in such a manner."

"You'll know the real worth of water when the well runs dry."

BENJAMIN FRANKLIN

Wealth

"If you want to be a millionaire, you have to think like one."

DR. JOHNNIE COLEMAN

"Do not be indifferent to money."

REVEREND IKE

"A person's true wealth is the good he/she does in the world."

MOHAMMED

Wickedness

"To see and listen to the wicked is already the beginning of wickedness."

CONFUCIUS

"A wicked man who reproaches a virtuous one is like one who looks up and spits at heaven; the spittle soils not the heaven, but comes back and defiles his own person."

THE BUDDHA

Will

"The saddest failures in life are those that come from not putting forth the power and will to succeed."

EDWIN PERCY WHIPPLE

"Man is made great or little by his own will."

JOHANN CHRISTOPH SCHILLER

"People do not lack strength; they lack will."

VICTOR HUGO

"A person with a half volition goes backwards and forwards and makes no way on the smoothest road but a man with a whole volition advances on the roughest and will reach his purpose if there be even a little wisdom in it."

THOMAS CARLYLE

"There is no such thing as a great talent without a great will."

HONORÉ BALZAC

"My will shall shape my future. Whether I fail or succeed shall be no man's doing but my own. I am the force; I can clear any obstacle before me or I can be lost in the maze. My choice, my responsibility-win or lose-, only I hold the key to my destiny."

ELAINE MAXWELL

Winners

"Winners do not go to a competition looking for a win. Winners go to a competition remembering how to win."

DENNIS WHEATLEY

Winning

"Winning isn't getting ahead of others. It's getting ahead of yourself."

ROGER STAUBACH

Wisdom

"Much wisdom often goes with fewest words."

SOPHOCLES

"In sickness, let me not say, 'am I getting better of my pain?' as I am getting better for it."

William Shakespeare

Wolves

"Wolves are not bad guys. They are just animals trying to figure out how to make a living." Animal rights advocate

Woman

"A beautiful woman is a jewel but a good woman is a treasure."

Saadi

"The most dangerous acquaintance a married woman can make is to have a female confidante."

Dorothée DeLuzy (French actress)

"Virtue, modesty and truth are the guardian angels of woman."

Caleb C. Colton

"A man without religion is to be pitied but a godless woman is a horror above all things."

Augusta Evans

"Men have sight; women have insight."

Victor Hugo

"Love which is only an episode in the life of a man, is the entire history of woman's life."

Madame de Staël

Worries

"As a cure for worries, work is better than whiskey."

THOMAS A. EDISON

Youth

"Youth is a wonderful thing. What a crime to waste it on children."

GEORGE BERNARD SHAW

"If a young man is loose in his principles and habits; if he lives without plan and without object, spending his time in idleness and pleasure, there is more hope of a fool than of him."

JOEL HAWES

"Youth is beautiful. Its friendship is precious. The intercourse with it is a purifying release from the worn and stained hardness of older life."

NATHANIEL PARKER WILLIS

Wisdom sayings – Ernest S. Merrill-Boyd

Part Two

"Don't visit your neighbour too often. He may get tired of you and come to despise you."

PROVERBS 25:17

"A rich man has many friends but a poor man is despiseth even by his own neighbours."

PROVERBS 14:20

"People learn from one another just as iron sharpens iron."

PROVERBS 27:17

"This is why I tell you: do not be worried about the food and drink you need in order to stay alive or about the clothes for your body. After all, isn't life worth more than food. And isn't the body worth more than clothes? Can any of you live a bit longer by worrying about it?"

MATTHEW 6: 25,27

"The Lord humbles those who are proud."

ISAIAH 26: 5

"Kind words bring life, but cruel words crush your spirit."

PROVERBS 15:4

"The start of an argument is like the first break in a dam; Stop it before it goes any further."

PROVERBS 17: 14

"Corrupt judges accept secret bribes and then justice is not done."

PROVERB 17:23

"Get good advice and you will succeed. Don't go charging into battle without a plan."

PROVERBS 20:18

"Sometimes it takes a painful experience to make us change our ways."

PROVERBS 20:30

"As he thinketh in his heart so is he."

PROVERBS 23: 7

"But if any provide not for his own and especially those of his own house, he hath denied the faith and is worse than an unbeliever."

1 TIMOTHY 5:8

"When evil men are in power, crime increases, but the righteous will live to see the downfall of such men."

PROVERBS 29: 16

"When good men come to power, every body celebrates but when bad men rule, people stay in hiding."

PROVERBS 28:12

"Show me a righteous ruler and I will show you a happy people. Show me a wicked ruler and I will show you a miserable people."

PROVERBS 29: 2

"When the king is concerned with justice, the nation will be strong but when he is concerned only with money, he will ruin his country"

PROVERBS 29: 4

"A false accusation is as deadly as a sword."

PROVERBS 25:18

"Poor people are the rich man's slave. Borrow money and you are the lender's slave."

PROVERBS 22:7

"Discipline your children while they are young enough to learn. If you don't you are helping them destroy themselves."

PROVERBS 19:18

"A gossip can never keep a secret. Stay away from people who talk too much."

PROVERBS 20:19

"Some men have power and others have to suffer under them."

ECCLESIASTES 8:9

"For sin is the breaking (transgression) of the law."

1 JOHN3:4

"The wicked runneth when no one pursueth."

PROVERBS 28:1

"We use the tongue to give thanks to our Lord and God our Father and also to curse our fellow men and women who are created in the likeness of God. Words of thanksgiving and cursing pour out from the same mouth. This should not happen. No spring of water pours out sweet water and bitter water from the same opening."

JAMES 3: 9 - 11

"Let us pray, not for lighter burdens but for stronger backs."

"Be with me Lord when I am in trouble."

Authors' Reference Index

Profile

Sulayman S. Nyang

Sulayman S. Nyang, a dear and loyal friend to the author, teaches at Howard University in Washington, D.C. where he serves as Professor of African Studies. From 1975 to 1978, he served as Deputy Ambassador and Head of the Chancery of the Gambia Embassy in Jeddah, Saudi Arabia. Following his diplomatic stint, he immigrated to the United States and returned to academic life at Howard University where he later assumed the position of department chair from 1986 to 1993. He also serves as co-director of Muslims in the American Public Square, a research project funded by The Pew Charitable Trusts.

Professor Nyang has served as consultant to several national and international agencies. He has served on the boards of the African Studies Association, the American Council for the Study of Islamic Societies and the Association of Muslim Social Scientists. He is listed on the editorial boards of several national and international scholarly journals. He has lectured on college campuses in Africa, Asia, Europe and the Americas.

Professor Nyang has written extensively on Islamic, African and Middle Eastern affairs. His latest book is entitled Islam in America. His best known works are Islam, Christianity and African Identity (1984), A Line in the Sand: Saudi Arabia's Role in the Gulf War (1995), co-authored with Evan Hendricks and Religious Plurality in Africa, co-edited with Jacob Olupona. His numerous scholarly pieces have appeared in African, American, European and Asian journals.

About the author

The author is a Caribbean national but who received his primary, secondary and tertiary education in the Caribbean, South America, the United States and Europe respectively and later, his spiritual and existential education in Antigua and Barbuda.

He is a multi-linguist, and a literary person by profession. He is a New York Times scholarship recipient; a summa cum laude graduate of Hampton University, a former Fellow at the University of Illinois at Champaign-Urbana and has pursued further studies at postgraduate level in Education at the University of Oxford, Educational Administration and Leadership at Miami University in Oxford, Ohio, and Foreign Language Curriculum Design at the University of the West Indies (Mona, Jamaica) in collaboration with the University of Concepción (Chile). He has been recognized by many institutions of higher learning for his remarkable contribution to the foreign language service and has received many awards from numerous educational institutions such as the Who's Who Among Students in American Universities and Colleges Award and the W. Adrian Freeman Fellowship Award for eminent scholarship.

He has also served in the educational system in the United States, the United Kingdom, Antigua and Barbuda, Dominica and Bermuda.

He has published in Time, Ebony, Newsweek International and Black World magazines. and Stockwell's Anthology of Poems (United Kingdom)

Wisdom Sayings For Our Troubling Times is his first published book.

Notes

Notes

Notes

Notes

Notes

www.ingramcontent.com/pod-product-compliance
Ingram Content Group UK Ltd.
Pitfield, Milton Keynes, MK11 3LW, UK
UKHW021053270726
13967UKWH00012B/646

9 781425 145460